Unspoken, Until Now

ISBN: 979-8-9957764-2-0
Published by The Olive Archives

Prologue: The Night Everything Shifted

I remember the sound before I understood the meaning: the crowd, the whistle, the pause that felt too long. My son had been hit before, but something about this one felt different. Not louder. Just heavier.

He sat there for what seemed like an hour before he finally stood up and walked off the field without a word.

No limp. No tears. No sign of frustration. Just silence.

That silence stayed with me. It followed us home. It lingered in the corners of our days, quiet but growing.

Looking back now, I realize that was the moment everything started to change, not just for him, but for all of us. It was the night I began to understand that strength isn't always about pushing through; sometimes it's about listening, even when you don't yet have the words for what you're hearing.

This story begins on a football field, but it's not about football It's about what happens after, when the lights fade, and you're left with the echoes of what no one talks about.

Foreword

This book wasn't something I ever planned to write.

But there came a point when silence no longer served my son or me. What we went through as a family wasn't easy to name, let alone explain. And for many Black families, we've been conditioned to keep it all inside. But what happens when keeping it in begins to cost us everything?

Our story begins on a football field, but this is not a story about football.

It's about what was changing underneath.

The things we couldn't see yet.

The signs we almost missed.

And the pain we didn't know how to name.

Unspoken Until Now is not a manual. It's not written by a professional or a scholar. It's written by a mother. One who loved her son through moments she couldn't understand.

One who stayed by his side when the world told him to toughen up. One who believes we need to start telling the truth about what it looks like to live, fight, and heal through mental illness, especially in our community.

If even one person finds clarity, comfort, or courage in these pages, then it was worth writing.

This is for the sons and the daughters.

The sisters and the brothers. The aunts, uncles, and cousins.

This is for the families who have stayed quiet too long. Let's speak now.

Chapter 1: The First Blow

He had always been a quiet, introverted, reserved, gentle kid in ways people didn't always expect from a boy. He wasn't loud. He didn't try to take up space. But his spirit? It was steady. Kind. Deep.

But when he was on the field, something clicked. Football was his language. Tackling people, reading the plays, pushing through—all of that made sense to him. He wasn't aggressive by nature, but on the field, he became something else: focused. Fierce. Free.

He loved it. He lived for it. There was pride in it, too, not just in the game but in what it gave him. Discipline. Brotherhood. Structure. Confidence.

Then came the first concussion. There was no stretcher. No dramatic fall. No crowd going silent. Just a hit. We did what we were told. Rest. Recover. Monitor symptoms. He was pulled from the next few games and kept under observation. And when the doctors cleared him, we exhaled.

So, we moved forward. Back to school. Back to football. Back to normalcy, or so we thought.

We didn't know it then, but the first concussion shifted something.

Arric: After the First Blow

I didn't even think of it as a concussion at first. I just knew my head hurt. I had to stay out for a few games to recover, and I didn't like that at all. I wanted to be out there with my team. I was used to playing almost the entire game, but now I'm on the sidelines, just watching.

Chapter 2: The Walk-Off

He returned to the game after that first hit. Played a few more games. Tried to push through like they told us to. The headache eventually faded, and to most people, that meant he was fine. Time passed and we started to believe it too.

He looked like himself again. Acted like himself. On the field and off.

And for a while, it felt like we were past it.

Then came the second blow.

I remember the moment because the air shifted. He tackled someone. Hard. The hit that makes everyone watching suck in their breath all at once. You could hear the helmets crack from the bleachers. A hush fell over the crowd, not the usual cheer or groan, just silence.

He sat there for a moment, then he walked off the field.

He didn't make a scene. He didn't fall apart. He just removed himself.

His coach was livid.

I don't know what went through his mind in that exact moment. But when he got up and walked off, despite being told to stay in, I knew something wasn't right.

We brought him in for tests. Followed every step. Ruled things out. Waited in hospital rooms with fluorescent lights and a growing uneasiness in my chest.

They ran the tests. Said everything looked normal. We were told more than once that the scans showed nothing alarming. The MRIs were clear; the CT scans were unremarkable.

But what they didn't tell us, or maybe what they couldn't explain, is that not all brain injuries leave visible marks. A concussion doesn't always bleed, it doesn't always swell, and it doesn't always announce itself on a screen. Sometimes it just changes your child. Quietly.

That's when everything we couldn't name began to show itself.

Not just his relationship with the game, but with himself. With his future. With the weight of trying to be "tough enough" in a world that already expects our black boys to be made of steel.

He stopped talking about football. School became harder. His moods became unpredictable. And I couldn't help but feel like we were watching something unravel slowly, quietly, and without a name.

He wasn't himself. Or maybe...he was becoming a new version of himself, one that had seen something, felt something, and didn't know how to put it into words yet.

So, we moved forward, slowly and cautiously, with this quiet, unnamed weight between us. Watching. Waiting. Hoping for signs of healing that no test could measure.

I didn't know then how much that walk off the field would come to symbolize everything that followed. The silent exit. The slow unraveling. The quiet ways trauma introduces itself.

Arric: The Day I Walked Off the Field

I played a few more games after the first concussion. I was getting back to my game, starting to feel like myself again. Then came the day everything shifted. It was a regular game. Nothing special. But the moment I tackled him, I knew something wasn't right, just a quiet, internal alarm. I didn't wait for someone to notice. I walked off because my head wasn't right. My body was moving, but my brain was somewhere else.

I just knew something was wrong, but my coach just wanted to win the game. He didn't ask how I felt. He just saw me walk off and took it personally. I didn't ask for permission. I didn't argue. I didn't wait. I knew I couldn't stay on the field, so I just walked off.

Chapter 3: The Couch

He had never lain on the couch before.

Not once. Not in his entire life. My son had always slept in his room, even when he wasn't feeling well.

So, when I came in and saw him there, just lying out on the couch, asleep, I knew something wasn't right.

At first, I thought he was just tired. Maybe just worn out. But something in my spirit told me to sit with him. I didn't wake him. I just sat nearby, watching the rise and fall of his chest, trying to quiet the uneasiness that had started to build in mine. When he finally stirred, I started asking questions. Nothing heavy, just light conversation, trying to gauge where he was. But his answers didn't make sense. He wasn't joking.

He was...unclear.

I walked him to his room, thinking he just needed rest. Maybe sleep would reset whatever was off.

I didn't know that night would be the beginning of everything shifting. Later, after I'd gone to bed, after the house had gotten quiet, he tried to leave. He had packed a bag and left the house. Thank God for Nick, the neighbor down the street, whom he had talked to before, and who happened to be outside that night. Nick is the reason my son came back into the house. Nick saw something I didn't. He talked to him. Talked him back inside.

The next morning, I saw Arric asleep on the couch again and the bags in the corner. I didn't understand. It didn't make sense. I was getting ready for work. His father was home. I thought we were okay. But we weren't.

Arric: Fight or Flight

I remember waking up and just...not feeling right. But not like a headache or being tired. It was like my brain wasn't connecting to anything.

I didn't feel like myself.

I started packing a bag. I wasn't trying to run away from home. I wasn't angry. I wasn't scared of anyone in the house. I just knew I couldn't stay still. I needed to move. I needed to get away from whatever was happening inside me.

That was fight or flight. And I chose flight.

But I didn't make it far. Nick saw me. He just started talking. Just talked to me like I was still human. And that was enough.

It was strange to be pulled back by words rather than by force. He didn't grab me, didn't yell. He just stood there like he saw me, even when I couldn't see myself. That's the only reason I walked back inside.

I eventually came back inside and lay on the couch. I didn't want to go back to my room. I didn't want to explain. I just wanted to be somewhere different. Somewhere softer.

I don't remember falling asleep. I remember the quietness around me.

Chapter 4: The ER Visit

The bags by the couch lingered in my mind as I tried to focus at work. I hadn't made sense of it yet, but I couldn't shake the feeling in my chest.

Then my phone rang. It was my husband.

His voice was tight. He said, "I'm taking him to the hospital. I don't know what's going on." No details. Just fear.

Those words hit like a wave. So, I did what any mother would do, I grabbed my things and rushed out the door.

When I got to the emergency room, I found my son lying in a hospital bed. Still. Quiet. Looking at the wall, or maybe not really looking at anything at all.

He wasn't talking. Nobody knew what was going on.

The nurses were asking questions. The doctors were trying to figure out what to assess. And my husband seemed irritated; he thought our son might be faking it, being dramatic and playing around. That this was just one of those moody teenage things.

Test after test. Person after person. They had him talk to different doctors, therapists, and evaluators, but none of it made much sense to me at the time. I was still trying to process what was even happening, still holding on to hope that this was something temporary. Something treatable.

Then the doctor came in. Calm. Professional. Detached, with words that stopped time.

"We believe your son is experiencing depression and anxiety...and possibly psychosis."

I remember blinking and staring at the doctor. Like they had spoken a language I didn't understand. *Psychosis? Depression?* And then it hit me hard, fast, and cold. This was real. This was happening. And I thought, *I'm going to lose my child.*

For a little while, I was angry with his father. Because he didn't see what I saw, he didn't feel what I felt. He had thought our son might be faking it. He's always been one of those *"suck it up and deal with it"* kind of men. Not because he doesn't care. But because that's how *he* was raised.

Push through. Don't complain. Don't cry. Just make it to the next day.

But this wasn't that. And I knew it.

I saw something shift in his face. He didn't say much. But I saw it. A kind of quiet understanding. A kind of guilt, maybe. Or maybe just fear. That moment when the strong one realizes that strength has nothing to do with pretending nothing's wrong.

And in that moment, something in him changed, too.

Arric: Inside the Fog

I remember lying in that bed and not knowing how to explain what was happening in my head. I didn't have the words. I didn't even feel like I was real.

I could hear everyone talking, could hear my parents arguing, but it was like I was far away. I wanted to say something. I think I did. But nothing felt real enough to hold on to.

It was like time was bending, like I had been stuck in the same moment for hours. The ceiling tiles started to blur together. My thoughts were racing and stopping all at once. I couldn't trust what I was seeing or even what I was thinking.

I wasn't asleep. But I couldn't stay fully awake either. It was like floating and falling at the same time.

Chapter 5: The Bed in Room 3

They moved him into the hospital's mental health wing. It didn't look like the rest of the hospital; it looked cold. No soft lighting. No pastel walls. No comforting posters. Just sterile. There was a stillness that was hard to explain. There was no real bed, just a big plastic structure bolted to the floor. No personal belongings. Just a room. A blanket. Four walls and occasional screams from other patients in the area, not normal. I kept thinking my son didn't belong here, but he did.

Since he was a minor, one of us had to stay with him. We didn't care because we didn't want to leave him anyway. We took turns, but at home neither could rest.

While there, I could sit inside the room or just outside of it. Sometimes he wanted me nearby. Sometimes he didn't.

There were moments when I sat inside, quiet, just being there so he wouldn't be alone. But other times, he'd ask me to leave. He couldn't explain why, and I didn't push. So, I'd move to the chair outside, right in the hallway, where I could still see him through the window.

There were times when Arric wasn't really there. His body was, but his mind had gone somewhere I couldn't follow. I'd look into his eyes and realize he wasn't looking at me, not really. He was looking past me or through me, as if I were invisible, as if everything were invisible.

And I hated it. Not because he scared me, but because he felt unreachable. Like, no matter what I said or did, I couldn't bring him back. There was something in them I'd never seen before. A vacancy. A quiet kind of emptiness that chilled me.

My son was still here, physically. But emotionally and mentally, he was lost. Lost within himself. And all I could do was sit on the other side of the glass, praying that somehow, he'd find his way back.

They told me the room he was in was temporary.

The doctors said they'd be making some calls. That they would look into transfer options. And just like that, they turned to me and asked where I wanted my son to go next.

As if I knew. As if I'd ever imagined having to choose a mental health facility for my child.

But there I was, sitting across from professionals asking for input, asking for decisions, while I was still trying to breathe through the fact that my son was in a locked psychiatric unit with a bed bolted to the floor.

I wanted to scream. I wanted to run. I wanted to wrap him up and take him home. But I knew he needed help I couldn't give him. Help he couldn't get from a blanket and a mother's arms alone.

When I finally made the decision, it felt like I had climbed a mountain to stand still.

• • • •

ARRIC: ROOM 3

That room didn't feel like a place for healing. It felt like a place where people were sent when they no longer made sense.

The silence in that room was loud. Not peaceful, just...empty.

I didn't feel crazy. But I didn't feel normal either. I just felt, gone. The bed was hard. The blanket was thin. The walls were blank. I stared at them for hours, trying to find patterns in the paint and trying to find something to hold on to.

Sometimes my mom sat in the corner. Quiet. Just breathing. I could feel her watching me. I didn't know how to explain what was happening in my head. I didn't have the words. I didn't even know if I was still me.

Other times, I asked her to leave. I didn't mean it in a mean way. I just needed space. Or silence. Or nothing. I didn't know what I needed.

Chapter 6: The Long Ride

The paperwork took forever. It was two days before the center had space and arranged transportation. I watched the clock tick past hours I couldn't name. Emotions twisted. I waited. I prayed. I tried not to fall apart.

When the ambulance finally arrived, they prepared to transport him. They strapped him in gently, like they were handling something fragile. They tried to make conversation, but he didn't respond.

That drive behind the ambulance was one of the longest of my life. I cried the whole way. Not loud. Not hysterical. Just steady tears that wouldn't stop falling.

I didn't know what would happen next. I didn't know if this place would help him. I didn't know if he'd come back to me whole. I just knew I had to keep going for him.

When we got to the treatment center, I sat in the lobby, eyes red, filling out more paperwork, talking to the staff, meeting new people, and watching my son sit in silence on another hospital bed, waiting to be admitted again.

He didn't talk much. He didn't ask questions. He just looked straight ahead. Still here. But still not himself.

I kept telling myself this was the right choice, but was it?

After the paperwork was signed and he was fully checked in, they escorted him back into the part of the treatment center I couldn't follow.

I stood there, watching them take him down a hallway I had never seen before. I didn't know what was on the other side. I didn't know who he'd be around, or what kind of care he would receive, or if he'd feel afraid.

I kept asking myself the question no mother ever wants to ask: Did I make the right decision?

Was this the right treatment center? Was this place going to help him or make him feel even more broken? Was he going to be protected?

Would they see him for who he really is? Would he know that I still loved him even from a distance?

So many questions. No real answers.

And when I walked out of that building, out into the parking lot, I sat in my car and cried. Not just a tear or two. I wept.

Because I had just left my baby behind. My child. The one who had never really been away from me for more than a night or two. And now he was going to be there for *weeks.* Maybe longer.

It broke something in me.

But I also knew I had done what I could. I had loved him the best I could. And even though I couldn't be in the room, I was with him in every way that mattered.

I hoped God, I prayed, that somewhere deep inside, he knew that.

That he felt my love still reaching him.

That when he closed his eyes at night, even in that unfamiliar place, he could still feel me holding him in prayer.

And then I drove home.

One of the longest drives of my life.

Not because of the distance. But because of all I was carrying during that ride.

Arric: Behind the Locked Door

I remember getting in the ambulance, but I really wasn't sure where I was going. When we got to the center, the questions started all over again.

Everyone kept talking around me, asking things, explaining things. I just wanted it all to stop. The noise. The questions.

When they closed the door behind me, I didn't cry. I didn't speak. I just went into my room, sat on the bed, and looked around. But even in that silence, I knew my mom was out there somewhere; I could still feel her energy through the walls.

She was there. Somewhere close. She was probably crying in the car again because I saw her eyes were red when they took me out of the ambulance.

Chapter 7: What a Mother Does

When I got home, I knew that I would need to gather a few things for him. Some personal items. Something familiar. Something that said, you are still you, even in this new place. I walked into his room and sat on the edge of his bed. The blanket was still rumpled from the last time he slept there. I didn't touch it. I just sat, letting the silence speak for both of us.

I called the nursing station every chance I could.

Every morning. Every afternoon. Every time I had a moment at work, between thoughts or tears. If I could've sat outside the unit and watched through the walls, I would've. But this was all I had, the phone.

So, I used it. I mean used it! I asked questions. Sometimes the same ones repeatedly.

"How is he doing today?"

"What are you giving him?"

"Did he eat anything this morning?"

"Is he opening up?"

"Did he go outside?" "Is he sleeping okay?" "Has anything changed since he went to sleep last night?"

I didn't care if they were tired of hearing from me. That was *my* child back there. And this was the only way I could reach him.

Sometimes they'd tell me, "He's quiet but cooperative." Sometimes, "He ate a little more today." Other times, "Still keeping to himself."

Every word mattered. Every little update became a thread I could hold onto.

I was trying to read between the lines, trying to hear my son inside those reports. Because when someone you love is behind locked doors, healing in a place you can't visit freely, you don't wait for answers to come to you. You call. You ask. You fight with your voice.

Because that's what a mother does.

Arric: She Never Let Go

I knew she was calling. I didn't always know the details, but I knew my mom was checking on me. I could feel it.

Sometimes I'd hear them say, 'Your mom called again.' And it would calm something in me I didn't even realize was tense. Like, even though I was locked in, I wasn't forgotten.

I was fighting on the inside, and my mom was fighting for me on the outside.

Chapter 8: Firsts and Fears

The first phone call from him was a relief I can't even explain. To *hear his voice,* to know he could talk again, to feel even the smallest piece of *him* returning, that gave me something I hadn't felt in days: hope.

He sounded like himself. Not fully, but enough. Enough to let me exhale a little. Enough to remember that he was still in there.

Then came the first in-person visit. Same thing. A glimpse. A piece of my baby. Still quiet. Still distant. But present.

And then came the aftercare conferences.

Family meetings. Doctor conversations. Long, clinical terms spoken gently but firmly. Descriptions of his condition. Updates on his progress, discussions about what to do next. We were two parents trying to look like we understood what was happening.

Then the words I didn't expect: "You'll need to remove all sharp objects from the home. Put away the knives. Hide medications. Lock up anything that could be harmful."

I just sat there. Trying to keep my face still. Trying not to let my stomach drop all the way to the floor.

Put the knives away?

I was still trying to process the fact that my child had been in the mental health center, and now I was being told how to "safety-proof" my own home, his home, as if it were dangerous to love someone going through this.

But this wasn't about fear. It was about preparation.

Because healing wasn't just about *getting him better*. It was about creating a new kind of environment. One that could hold him when things got heavy again.

Later that evening, the knives were removed, and extra locks were added to the doors. I didn't say anything; I couldn't deal with it. My heart was aching.

But because I knew what it meant. We were no longer just parents. We were guardians of his safety, even from himself.

Arric: Our Phone Call

"I didn't know what to say. I just missed my mom. And I could tell by her voice that she missed me, too. Her voice was comforting. It reminded me of home. Of warmth. Of safety. Of being seen. I knew, if I was broken…I was still hers. Still loved. Still wanted. Still worth something. Even behind locked doors. Even in a place where everything felt unfamiliar. Even when I didn't feel like myself.

She didn't say anything profound. She just stayed on the line. Breathing with me. Holding space. And that was enough."

It felt like prayer without words, like just hearing her breathe on the other end was proof that I wasn't gone completely. It was proof that no matter how far away my mind felt, I was still tethered to her.

Chapter 9: Preparing His Room

Back at home, I went to his room.

It was messy, just like you'd expect a teenage boy's room to be. Clothes on the floor. Random things out of place. His shoes were the only thing neatly placed away. Nothing out of the ordinary for his room...except that *he wasn't in it.*

And that made everything feel different.

So, I cleaned it.

At first, I told myself it was to straighten things up. I wanted him to come home to a clean room. A fresh space. Some sense of peace waiting for him on the other side of this.

But if I'm honest, I was doing more than cleaning. I was looking. Looking for answers. Looking for signs I might have missed. Looking for anything that could explain what was happening.

I didn't find any notes. No messages. No clues.

Just silence.

Still, I washed and folded his clothes. I made his bed. I cleared the top of his dresser. Because even though I couldn't be there with him, I could do *this.*

And I had to pack his things- gather some clothes, shoes without laces, and personal items. Things that might bring him a small piece of comfort where he was.

Things to remind him who he was.

And maybe...remind *me* too.

I stood there for a moment, holding his hoodie in my hands longer than necessary, before placing it in the bag.

Then I added a book.

And inside, I slipped a note.

Something simple. Something he could hold onto.

Because I needed him to feel me... even when I couldn't be there.

Arric: My Room, My Reality

I thought about my room while I was away. Not because I missed the mess, but the bed I was lying in at the center wasn't mine. But my room back home was mine. That was where I knew who I was.

Not just because of my things, but because of what it held: Memories.

Peace.

A sense of control in a world that suddenly felt uncontrollable.

I used to complain about having to clean it. But now all I wanted was to be in it.

Not to hide, but to feel real again.

Chapter 10: Home

Once he was released with the medication, the plan, the instructions, we felt something we hadn't felt in weeks: hope.

When he finally came home, I watched him walk into his room like someone returning to a place they weren't sure still existed.

When he went inside his room, I saw his eyes scan the bed, the dresser, and the folded clothes. The stitch stuffed animal sitting in the middle-a small, familiar thing in a world that had felt anything but familiar. He was back in his space. And somehow, I hoped, that meant he was back in himself.

He talked more.

He ate.

He slept. We exhaled. We had hope again.

But then...things turned quickly.

After just two days, we were back in that place. Another set of questions from intake personnel I wished we didn't need to answer again.

And this time, it hit harder. Because this time, we *had* the plan. We *had* the diagnosis. We were doing everything right.

So why were we back?

It felt like failure. Like everything we did wasn't enough. Like everything *he* was doing wasn't enough.

And I sat there thinking, *I'm going to lose my son.*

Not because he wasn't strong. Not because he wasn't loved. Not because we didn't try.

But because sometimes the fight for mental health isn't one battle, it's a war. And even when you're fighting together, it still feels like you're losing ground.

I was tired. He was tired. We refused to give up. Even when it didn't seem to be enough.

Arric: The Second Time Was Harder

Going back felt worse than the first time. Like everything I did to get better didn't count.

I didn't want to go back. Not because I didn't want help. But because I felt like I had already tried.

I was taking the meds. I was doing the work. I was doing what they said. And I still ended up there.

But I also knew something wasn't right, and I just wanted it to stop. So, I walked down the hall away from my mom, ready to try again.

Chapter 11: In the Middle of It All

My Reflection: Learning What I Didn't Know

No one prepares you for the kind of love that breaks and binds you at the same time. Motherhood, they say, is strength, sacrifice, and softness. But what they don't say is this:

Sometimes motherhood is a silent scream. Sometimes it's signing your name on a paper that says, please take care of my child because I no longer know how.

Sometimes it's grieving a version of your child you thought you knew, while holding hope for the one still fighting their way back.

Mental illness didn't ask me if I was ready to become this kind of mother.

It didn't wait for the holidays to pass. It didn't matter that I had held him as a baby, kissed his knees when he fell, or knew the smell of his skin after a nap.

It came anyway. And yet, so did I. Every day after that moment, I showed up with my fear, my ache, my faith, and my stubborn hope.

Because that's what mothers do. Even when no one claps. Even when no one understands. Even when we break.

The word that scared me the most was psychosis.

I knew about depression and anxiety. But this word, this diagnosis, was foreign and frightening. So I did what mothers do when they're scared, I started searching for answers.

I read everything I could. I asked questions repeatedly to understand what we were facing. What this meant for him. What this meant for us.

Because when the doctors told me to remove sharp objects from the house, they weren't saying my son had tried to hurt himself. They were telling me that psychosis can alter how a person sees the world. That it can make you question what's real or imagine things that aren't. Psychosis doesn't mean someone is dangerous. But that it distorts your sense of safety, of memory, of logic, without warning, so safety plans matter.

And that shook me.

So, I prepared. I studied.

I learned everything I could, not because I wanted to know, but because I had to.

I wanted to be ready for when he came home. Ready to care. Ready to notice. Ready to respond with love instead of fear.

I remember the day he said he wanted to live with his dad. It caught me off guard, not because I didn't understand, but because I did. He wanted to know that part of himself, the part that had always felt slightly out of reach.

These days, our paths look different now, but I believe we both still hope they lead back to the same love, the love that built this family and keeps carrying it forward.

Time softened a lot between them- not in grand gestures, but in small ones. A text here. A visit there. A few more conversations that didn't end in silence. It's not the picture-perfect bond people imagine, but it's a bridge being built brick by brick, on both sides. Healing rarely looks like what we expect. Sometimes it's quieter, slower, but just as sacred.

Big Brother's Reflection

After his first hospitalization, when we'd be driving somewhere, he'd point out a car and say, *"That one's following us."* I didn't see it, but he believed it.

There were times he told me the doctors and people at the hospital were out to get him. He didn't trust anyone; he said the meds were trying to control him.

Back then, Arric and I didn't really talk much. As kids, we weren't close- the age gap between us was too wide. We started talking more after all this happened. I used to think, *maybe if we'd been closer, he would've listened to me.*

I don't know if he actually would have, but I wish I'd tried more. I wish he'd had somebody to talk to, to get what was going on in his head out in the open.

I remember seeing a video of Arric in the hospital, a blanket pulled up over him. At first, I didn't even realize what I was seeing. Then it hit me, he was really in there, really going through it. That's when I understood it was deeper than I thought. But I didn't ask too many questions.

Another time, when we went for a drive, he kept looking around, saying people were following him. I told him, *"Bro, just relax. If someone were following us, I'd feel it too."* But he couldn't relax. He was seeing something else, something we couldn't see.

That was hard, watching him think the world was after him and not being able to convince him otherwise. And I didn't want to say too much, afraid he'd think I was part of it too.

If I could go back, I'd talk to him more. Even if he didn't want to listen. Even if he didn't believe me. I'd still talk, so that he knew somebody was trying.

A Father Reflects

I won't lie, I didn't take it seriously at first. I thought he was just being dramatic, and that his mom was babying him. Maybe he was trying to get out of school or something.

I grew up in a time when you didn't talk about feelings; you just handled them.

So, when I saw him on the couch that day, slipping away in front of me, I didn't know what I was looking at. I thought he'd snap out of it.

But after rushing him to the hospital and seeing him in that hospital bed, quiet, distant, still, my whole mindset shifted.

I know I talk a lot. I always have. I wasn't the type to yell, and I didn't like punishing him to punish him. But if something went wrong, I'd sit him down, and he knew he was in for it. I'd give the whole speech.

I wanted him to understand. To think about things. Not just say "sorry" and move on.

Truth is...the lecture was the punishment. And yeah, they could go long. I wasn't trying to wear him down, but I probably did a few times.

Since then, I've had to unlearn a lot. I've had to listen more. Speak less. I've had to watch my son fight battles I never saw coming. Battles I couldn't fix with a speech.

I don't always get it right. I may not always know what to say. But I'm here for him. And I'm proud of the way he's fighting.

There are stories where a father loses a close, loving relationship with his child because of mental illness. This isn't one of those stories. The truth is, my son and I never had that kind of bond.

Even before the signs of his mental health struggles appeared, there was a quiet distance between us. I don't know exactly when or where it started. Maybe it was how we were both wired. Maybe it was the weight of things we never learned how to name. Maybe life didn't give us the soil we needed to grow something steady.

Whatever it was, our connection always felt just out of reach.

But that doesn't mean I didn't love him. I did; fiercely, quietly, sometimes clumsily, but always with hope. Hope that with time, healing, or grace, we might learn how to meet in the middle. That we'd find a way to be father and son in a way that worked for us.

Mental illness didn't take a beautiful bond away. It just reminded me how fragile unbuilt bridges can be and how much I still hope to cross one someday.

Kamira's Reflection: Loving Through the Storm

Watching someone you love go through something you can't fix is heartbreaking. Being with Arric while he was going through the toughest parts was emotionally heavy, but my first response was to pray. I felt sadness, yes, but more than anything, I had this deep desire to understand what he was going through mentally.

I took the time to really learn him, and in doing that, I adapted. I grew in patience, in awareness, and in love. It wasn't easy, but it opened my eyes to parts of him and myself I never truly saw before. I wanted to help, to support him spiritually and emotionally, even when things felt uncertain. It was a time of reflection, patience, and faith, and it made me love him even more because I saw not just his struggle, but his strength.

Tara's Reflection: Us vs. The World

I've always been more than a sister to my brother; I've been his second mom. From the day he was born, I felt a pull to protect him, to guide him.

I wanted to be the one to teach him how to ride a bike, to tie his shoes, to face the world. Even when our parents stepped in, my instincts told me, no...let me handle this.

That's what happens when you grow up the oldest...you take on a role you never applied for, but one you can't imagine living without.

The day I realized something was deeply wrong with him didn't start with flashing alarms. It was just a regular day. I was sitting in the living room when he came downstairs, wearing nothing but his boxers, eyes dull and unfocused. He didn't speak, just glanced at me before walking outside.

It was pouring rain, the kind that soaks you through in seconds. At first, I thought maybe he was grabbing a package or picking up a DoorDash order.

But when minutes passed, and he didn't return, something in me, that unshakable big sister instinct screamed: Find him. I didn't think about shoes, or the rain, or anything else.

I just ran out into the street, calling his name repeatedly. "Arric! Arric!"

My feet slapped against the pavement, soaked within seconds. The rain blurred my vision, but I kept calling his name, louder each time.

Each time I called, the sound felt more desperate, my voice sharper. I finally spotted him sitting in the driver's seat of an old car he used to work on, now belonging to a neighbor.

He was motionless, staring into nothing. When I opened the door and took his arm, he didn't resist, but he didn't really come with me either.

It felt like I was guiding a ghost back home.

I told my mom immediately, "Something's wrong with Arric." And deep down, I knew this was different from his usual quirks or randomness.

I didn't know what was happening. I'd seen what being laced could do. A classmate in high school had been poisoned with rat-laced weed, and he was never the same. I wasn't going to let that happen to my brother. I needed him to laugh again, to burst into my room uninvited to say, "T, I need this," or "T, come see this."

I needed proof that the person I grew up with was still in there. The road to getting him back was a blur...frustrating, terrifying, and exhausting.

When he was admitted to the mental hospital, I wasn't allowed to go with my mom to take him. That tore me apart. I wanted to be there to ask the questions others were too scared to ask, to make sure every choice about his care was the right one. Instead, I sat at home, feeling like the one person who knew him best was being shut out of his fight.

We'd fought demons together before...this one was just bigger, louder, and meaner.

And there was another layer to it, my brother had a baby on the way. I kept thinking, how do you protect someone who's about to become someone else's protector?

The doctors kept changing his medication, trying to find the right balance, but to me, it felt like every change knocked him further off center. And while the center was trying to treat him medically, at home, extra locks were placed on doors, and knives were locked up. But me,

I never locked my door. His room was right next to mine, and I slept soundly knowing that no matter how lost he was in his mind, he would never hurt me.

I remember one time he wandered into a school, saying he wanted to check it out for his unborn child. That scared me in ways I can't even explain. The world is already dangerous for a black man, and with his mental state spiraling, I feared I'd get a call one day that he'd been shot during one of his roaming episodes.

Some days he'd seem like himself again. Then the fog would roll back in, and I'd see that lost look in his eyes. But I always saw a piece of him in there, enough to keep me from ever giving up.

I even started imagining a future where I'd have space in my own home for him, permanent and safe, a space where he's not a patient, not a case, just my brother.

Each time he asked to be checked back into the hospital, it broke my heart. But I also knew it meant he was still fighting...fighting for his mind, his dreams, his personality.

We talk about "life support" like it only applies to physical survival, but my brother was on a different kind of life support. He was battling for his mental life, and his choice to keep seeking help told me he wasn't ready to lose.

Tragedy can either break a family apart or bring them closer. I think ours broke, but when we put the pieces back together, the picture was clearer, stronger, and more beautiful than before.

We learned how to listen without fixing. How to sit in silence without rushing to fill it. Because when you've walked through fire together, you don't come out untouched. But you do come out forged.

And through it all, one thing has never changed: It's still my brother and me.

Us vs. them. Us vs. the world.

Arric: Through My Eyes, Then and Now

I wasn't always able to say it. And I definitely didn't always act like it. But I knew. I knew they were there.

My parents are doing the best they can.

My sister is checking on me in her own way. My brother is giving space but watching. Kamira is trying to hold everything together for our son and still not giving up on me.

It meant more than I could say. When your mind is loud, and the world doesn't make sense, but having people who stay, people who don't leave just because you're not "you," that's everything.

I didn't always show it. I didn't always say thank you. But I saw it. And I carry it with me now.

Sometimes, reading what everyone else remembers about those moments makes me wonder what I would've said if I had the words back then. I know they were scared, I was scared, too.

But fear doesn't always look the same on the outside. Mine looked like silence. Like anger. Like sleeping too much. Like walking away. I wasn't trying to be distant. I couldn't hold all of what was happening in my mind and explain it to someone else at the same time. So I shut down. Because staying quiet was so much easier than saying, "I'm lost, and I don't know what's real."

I heard things later, like how my dad didn't get it at first, but was there, and how my mom had to become an overnight expert. How Kamira prayed and held the pieces of everything together. How my siblings were holding space for me.

And it makes me feel one thing: grateful. Because even when I didn't see myself clearly, they still did. Even when I didn't reach for them, they reached for me. Even when I wasn't easy to love, they didn't stop trying.

I think about my dad's words, the part about bridges. He's not wrong; we weren't close. We didn't have the kind of bond people write about in poems or healing books. There were times, quiet moments, when I wished it were different. When I watched other fathers and sons laugh or argue or just be, and I'd feel this ache, wondering what it would've been like to have that kind of connection.

Most days, it felt like we were sharing air, not a life. But I love him. And maybe that's reason enough to try. There was even a time, after one of my lowest points, when I told Mom I wanted to go live with him. I thought maybe that would fix something in me or help us find our way back to each other. But he wasn't ready.

I understand now, but back then, it felt like being turned away from a place I was finally brave enough to reach for. That moment stuck with me-it built a quiet wall I didn't even realize was there. I think that's when I stopped expecting closeness and started settling for distance.

I think that's the part that hurts the most. Not that the bridge crumbled, but that maybe it never even had the foundation it needed. But foundations can be built. Bridges can be repaired. It might not look like the ones other people have, and it's not supposed to. What matters is that it's ours, built in our way, in our time. It might take longer than we'd like, but I believe there's still a way to make it happen.

Even if it starts with small steps, a conversation, a shared moment, a memory retold, it's something. And something is better than nothing.

Now that I have a son of my own, I think about that bridge more than ever. Before he was born, I wondered if my struggles would spill over onto him, if my shadows would swallow the light I wanted for his world. But then I met him. And in that moment, I realized fatherhood isn't about starting perfect; it's about starting and being present. It's about choosing, repeatedly, to show up.

I want to build something different with him, something solid, something soft at times. I don't always know how. I still battle my own shadows. But fatherhood has made me fight harder, because I see in his eyes the kind of trust you can't buy and can't fake.

Every time I hold him, or whisper "I love you," or sit quietly while he plays beside me, I feel like I'm laying down the first strong brick of our bridge. A bridge that will carry him toward the man he's meant to be.

Chapter 12: Why Him?

This kid, my son, is one of the sweetest kids you'll ever meet.

He doesn't love halfway. If he's your friend, you've got him for life. He'll care for you deeply, stand beside you, remember things you thought he forgot. He's loyal in a quiet, powerful way. And when it comes to family? He feels it all.

So, I couldn't help but ask, why him?

Why does someone so kind, so thoughtful, so full of heart have to carry *this*?

Why does *my baby,* who never caused trouble, who just wanted to be understood, have to go through *all of this*?

And I couldn't stop the questions in my head...

Did I pass this down to him? Is this my fault? Did my anxiety become his burden?

And I thought about all the years I lived with mine silently. All the times I pushed through without saying anything. All the patterns I might've passed down not just genetically, but emotionally. And it crushed me.

Because even though I know deep down that mental health challenges are no one's fault, it felt like mine. It felt like I gave him a wound I never meant to give.

I replayed moments from his childhood. The times I was too tired to engage. The days I was too anxious to be present. The ways I might've taught him, without meaning to, that silence was strength and struggle was private.

But I now know this: Love didn't cause this. Kindness didn't cause this. Being a quiet, beautiful soul didn't cause this.

And neither did I.

Mental illness doesn't choose based on goodness. It doesn't care how gentle you are, how loyal, how loved. It just arrives. Uninvited. Unfair.

But what we do next, that's where love shows up.

We are both living with things we didn't choose. But we're learning how to walk through them. Together.

Not perfectly. Not without pain. But with honesty. With grace. With a kind of love that doesn't ask *why*, but says *I'm here.*

Arric: Mom, This Isn't Your Fault

I know you hurt when I hurt, but know this isn't your fault.

You didn't give me this. You gave me love. You gave me safety. You gave me someone who sees me, really sees me, even when I don't make sense to myself.

It's just part of what I'm walking through.

And if anything, I'm glad it's you walking beside me.

Because you don't judge me. You don't treat me like I'm fragile. You treat me like I matter. Like I'm still me.

So, if you ever wonder if you failed me, you didn't.

You showed up. You stayed. You loved me through the fog. And that means more than you'll ever know.

Chapter 13: Generational Mental Health: Breaking the Quiet Cycle

Mental health challenges don't always start with us, but they often echo through us. In my family, silence was the default. We came from strong women who carried more than they ever said out loud. Women who prayed hard, worked harder, and cried quietly behind closed doors. Men who pushed through without naming their wounds, because no one ever gave them the space to pause.

We learned early that survival was the goal. Not healing. Not rest. Not honesty. Just surviving.

I grew up watching people hold pain like it was a secret inheritance. We inherited their strength, yes, but also their silence. And silence has a cost.

Because silence doesn't erase the wound, it passes it on.

People who never learned the words for what they were feeling, so they passed down the silence instead.

I watched my own mother push through exhaustion with a smile, never admitting that she was crumbling inside. And me? I learned to keep moving. To smile when I was unraveling inside. To "handle it." And when I became a mother, I carried those lessons with me, until life demanded something different. Until my son's pain showed me that silence wasn't strength at all. It was a weight, one that could crush us if we didn't set it down.

We come from a long line of survivors. But survival and healing are not the same thing. Surviving means you make it through. Healing means you learn to breathe again without holding your breath.

For generations, we didn't have the language. They didn't say words like "anxiety" or "depression." They said things like "I'm just tired" or "God will make a way."

And while faith did sustain us, silence also cost us. It costs us understanding. It cost us chances to break free earlier. It cost us the ability to see patterns that were passed down quietly, invisibly, from one generation to the next.

It's easy to dismiss what we didn't name.

But what we don't name, we often repeat.

Breaking that cycle doesn't mean blaming; it means choosing compassion over silence.

It means saying, "It's okay not to be okay," out loud.

It means healing for ourselves and for those who never got the chance.

We're not just surviving anymore. We're learning. We're talking. We're changing the story.

Breaking the cycle doesn't mean dishonoring the ones who came before us. It means honoring their survival while choosing a different path. It means saying, "It's okay to talk about this now. It's okay to name it. It's okay to heal." And for me, breaking the cycle began with telling my son, "You don't have to carry this alone."

Let's talk about it. Gently. Boldly. Together.

With open hands, open hearts.

Chapter 14: Safe Away from Home

There was only one treatment center I truly trusted. And more importantly, he trusted it.

They knew him. They remembered his name. He felt seen there. He wasn't just a number, a chart, or a problem to manage. He was *Arric.* And they treated him like that mattered. They saw past the diagnosis and into the person.

So, whenever something started to spiral again, that's where I called first. That's where I hoped we'd end up.

And I hated, hated, when they didn't have space. It was like someone pulling away the last safety net we had. Like watching the only lifeboat drift out of reach as the storm picks up again.

I remember once, I called, and they told me: "We don't have a bed for him right now...but if we have to, we'll put a mattress in the day room."

And I cried. Not because of the mattress. But because they *got it.*

Because they knew. They knew how much I needed to know he'd be in a place where he could breathe. Where I could, too.

Because when your child is in crisis, you don't just need treatment. You need trust. You need to know that the people caring for him see what you see. That they'll protect what you love. That they'll hold space for his healing, not just manage his symptoms.

That center became more than a facility. It became a lifeline. A place where he felt safe enough to be honest. Where he could say, "I'm not okay," and be met with compassion instead of confusion.

And every time we had to go back, it didn't feel like failure. It felt like choosing safety, choosing care, and choosing to keep fighting.

Even when the world outside didn't understand. Even when the system felt too big, too slow, too broken.

We had one place. One team. One space where he could be more than his pain.

And that made all the difference.

Arric: The Only Place That Felt Like Healing

I don't know how to explain it, but that place felt...calmer.

They didn't look at me like I was broken. They didn't talk at me. They talked to me.

I could tell they actually cared. Like, when they asked how I was doing, they waited for the answer. They remembered my name. They remembered what I said the day before.

Other places felt cold, like I was just a problem to fix or something to contain.

But this place... This place felt made for people like me. Not to erase what we were going through, but to remind us that we still mattered.

Chapter 15: The Wrong Place

During one crisis, the treatment center we trusted, the one that truly knew how to care for him, was full. We didn't have a choice. He had to be transferred somewhere else. And on paper, it was a treatment facility. But in reality, it didn't feel like treatment at all.

At first, he checked in, and things seemed okay. I tried to stay hopeful. I tried to convince myself that maybe this one would work too. Maybe I was just being overly protective. But then the phone rang.

It was him.

His voice cracked as he said, *"Mom, come get me, I can't stay here."*

Even in the middle of what he was battling, he knew. He knew his environment. He knew what didn't feel right. He knew this place wasn't going to help him heal. And I could hear it in his voice, the desperation, the exhaustion, the deep discomfort.

I didn't hesitate. I told them I was on the way. I couldn't get there fast enough.

He reached for me, even through his pain. And I reached right back.

That day reminded me: not all help is created equal. Just because a place is called a treatment center doesn't mean it's the right one. And the ones who are hurting the most can often feel the difference before anyone else does.

They know when a space is safe. They know when it's not. And we have to listen.

Because healing isn't just about medication or protocol, it's about dignity. It's about trust. It's about being seen.

And that day, my son saw clearly. Even through the fog. Even through the pain. He knew what healing didn't feel like.

And I'm grateful he spoke up. Grateful he reached out. Grateful we got him out.

Because sometimes, the bravest thing you can do is say, *"This isn't helping me."* And sometimes, the most important thing you can do is believe them.

Arric: One Call Away

I don't remember everything about that place, but I remember how it felt.

It felt cold, even when the temperature wasn't. It felt loud in a way that made it hard to think, but also too quiet in the wrong ways. It didn't feel safe. Not the safe where you can breathe and try to get better.

I didn't want to call my mom, but I knew I had to. Because if I stayed, I wasn't sure what would happen to me. And she answered, just like always. She didn't ask a million questions. She didn't hesitate. She just said, "I'm coming."

Chapter 16: Wrong, Again

Once again, due to limited space, my son had to be admitted to a different treatment center, one we didn't know, one that wasn't our preference. I tried to keep calm and trust the process, but deep down, I always worried more when he wasn't in the care of those we had grown to trust.

That unfamiliarity sat heavy on me. Because when you've finally found a place that understands your child, that sees them beyond the diagnosis, anything outside of that feels like a risk.

In the middle of the night, my phone rang. That kind of ring that doesn't feel normal. The one your spirit recognizes before your mind catches up.

It was a hospital.

Not the treatment center, but the emergency room. They said my son had been brought in, but everything after that is still a blur in my mind. I don't remember what I asked or hanging up the phone. I tossed on whatever I could, grabbed my keys, and ran out the door.

My heart was pounding. My thoughts were racing. And all I could think was Lord, please be with him. Because in that moment, I didn't know what had happened or what condition he was in. I didn't know if he was scared or if he even understood what was happening to him.

• • • •

ARRIC: TOO MUCH, TOO Fast

I knew something was off. Not just with me, but with the people and the place.

It felt rushed from the start. Nobody explained much.

They just gave me pills.

I didn't know what they were. I didn't know what they were supposed to do. I started to feel dizzy, then I passed out.

Chapter 17: Fourteen Floors

By the time I got to the hospital, they were already preparing to transfer him to be admitted to a different hospital that had a mental health floor that specialized in medical treatments for adolescents.

We ended up spending several days there; I learned the treatment center gave him more medication than he needed, and they wanted to keep him for observation. Days that were long, exhausting, filled with questions and unknowns. I was tired. He was tired.

And I hated when the doctors asked the same questions over and over.

"Is he suicidal? Any homicidal thoughts?" As if those were the only questions that mattered. As if depression only counted when it was loud and dangerous. But what about the kind that was quiet and consuming? The kind that didn't show up in threats or plans, but in the slow disappearance of the person you love.

Arric wasn't suicidal.

He wasn't homicidal.

He was just...suffering.

And I wanted someone to see that.

I *was* worried every single day. I worried because I could see what they couldn't. The stillness in him that wasn't peace. The silence that wasn't calm. The smile, when it showed up, didn't touch his eyes.

Major depression had wrapped itself around my son so tightly that I could barely remember the last time he felt light. I'm not talking about laughter- though that was rare, too. I mean lightness. The absence of weight. Of worry. Of fight.

And the truth is, I didn't know what else to do. I was showing up. I was loving him. I was trying everything I could. But I didn't know how to make it let go. Didn't know how to get him back.

And then came a moment I'll never forget.

I had stepped out, just for a moment, to go down to the cafeteria and grab something to eat. I took the elevator down, and as soon as I reached the lower level, I heard an overhead announcement. It included his room number.

I froze. My stomach dropped.

I didn't wait for the rest of the message; I turned around and sprinted back to the elevator. The doors felt like they took forever to close, and even longer to reopen. I ran down the hallway to his room.

He wasn't there. I looked at the sitter, at the nurses' station, at the security desk, desperate for someone to explain. No one could.

He had left. No one knew how or when, and no one could tell me where he had gone.

And at that moment, I couldn't breathe. The hallway seemed to tilt. I could hear my own heartbeat in my ears. That fear, the kind that only a parent knows when your child is missing, vulnerable, and hurting, took over. I was running on fumes and prayer.

The hospital staff who were supposed to watch him, monitor him, and protect him failed him, failed us.

He had walked out of the hospital past the very sitter who was assigned to watch him.

Elevators. Hallways. Security doors. Staff at their desks. Cameras.

And no one asked a question.

I know mistakes happen. But this wasn't a mistake. This was negligence. This was incompetence.

It wasn't just a system failure. It was a failure to *see* him.

He wasn't loud. He was hurting. And somehow, that made him invisible.

He was gone, hurt, confused, and alone.

As a first responder, my instinct was to call the police. But in that split second, something stopped me. I've seen how encounters with people in crisis can go wrong, the headlines, the footage, the names that never should've been lost.

Not because they were violent. Not because they were dangerous.

But because they were Black, unwell, and in the wrong place at the wrong time, and I was terrified that it could be my son. What do you do when the very system you serve might harm the person you love most?

It felt like forever before I heard that he had been found.

Found outside. He had walked right past the person assigned to watch him and made it from the 14th floor all the way down and outside the hospital.

Fourteen floors!

They didn't just guide him back inside. They had to struggle to bring him back. Because again, psychosis. Not because he was dangerous, but because in his mind, going back inside wasn't safe.

He wasn't just walking.

He was disconnected and caught in a reality that made sense only to him in that moment. His mind wasn't grounded in the same place as everyone else's. And trying to convince someone in psychosis to return to a place that feels threatening or unfamiliar can feel like chasing a shadow.

He didn't want to come back.

Not because he didn't love me. Not because he didn't want to get better.

But because in his mind, something else was happening. Something we couldn't see.

And that made everything ten times harder.

By the time they got him back inside, my emotions were everywhere: grief, fear, anger, relief, all tangled together. And the guilt...the guilt of stepping away for even a moment. The guilt of trusting a hospital that didn't see him. That didn't protect him.

I didn't know whether to scream, cry, or collapse.

But I knew this: Depression and psychosis may have had a hold on my child, but so did I. And I refused to let go.

Because love doesn't clock out, it doesn't wait for the system to catch up. It doesn't ask for permission to protect. It just shows up, repeatedly, even when the elevator doors take too long, even when the world feels tilted, even when the people meant to help forget how to see.

I saw him. And I will keep seeing him until the rest of the world learns how.

Arric: The Walk

I didn't know where I was going. I just knew I had to go.

I was tired of being there, in that room, hearing all those people outside, getting checked on. The air felt heavy, like every breath had to fight its way out. I wanted fresh air. My thoughts kept looping, speeding up, then stopping, then starting again, until I couldn't tell what was real and what wasn't. I needed out of the room, the building, my thoughts.

So, I got up. I walked out. No one stopped me.

Not the sitter who was supposed to be watching. Not the people at the nurses' station. Not security. Not anyone.

When I walked out, no one said anything. No one asked where I was going. I didn't sneak. I didn't hide. I just left. When they found me, I didn't understand what the big deal was. I wasn't trying to hurt anybody. I couldn't stay.

The Space Between

HEALING DOESN'T HAPPEN in one moment. It happens in the space between the moments, in the deep breaths, the small prayers, the quiet remembering that even broken things can still bloom.

Chapter 18: Doing the Work

It's been a while since the last inpatient stay. Thank God. Knock on wood. And anything else you can think of.

He's been doing the work. And I've seen it.

He knows more about himself than anyone, what he needs, what he feels, when something's shifting. And I've learned, too.

I know what to look for now. he way he eats. The way he sleeps. The way he moves through the room. The quiet signs. The invisible warnings. The little things that tell me what his baseline is, and when we're drifting from it.

I've learned how to watch. How to act. How to help him stay grounded before he ever has to go back.

We are not where we were. We are still healing. But we're walking forward, together.

Arric: Still learning, Still Here

It's not perfect. But it's better. I've learned how to pay attention to myself. Not just when things get bad, but before they do. I've learned how to check in with my thoughts. How to be honest about how I'm feeling, even if I don't always have the words right away.

I've learned that needing help doesn't make me weak; it makes me aware. It means I care about staying well. It means I've grown.

Sometimes I catch the signs early: the sleep changes, the noise in my head, the feeling like something's "off."

I tell my mom, I tell Aiden's Mom, I tell myself, or I tell other family members. I don't wait for it to crash.

There are still hard days. But they don't take me out like they used to. Because now I have tools. I have people. I have proof that I can come back from the dark.

And I don't take that for granted.

And I know not every day will be like this. But I'm holding onto those that are. Because it means I'm still here. Still healing. Still capable of joy.

Chapter 19: Looking Back to See Forward

It's strange how healing sneaks up on you.

Not all at once. Not in dramatic breakthroughs. But in quiet moments. In the way you breathe easier. In the way you sleep through the night. In the way you stop bracing for the worst.

I look back now, and I see the trail we've walked, the hills we climbed, and the storms we braved.

The hospital rooms. The phone calls. The missed diagnoses. The right ones. The wrong places. The good days. The terrifying ones.

I see the version of me that didn't know what to ask. The version of him that didn't know how to speak. And I see how far we've come.

We've learned the language of healing. We've learned how to name things. How to listen. How to stay. And even though we're still walking, we're walking with more light.

More tools. More truth. More trust.

I used to think healing meant going back to who we were before. But now I know, healing means becoming someone new. Someone softer. Stronger. Wiser.

We're not done. But we're not broken.

We are all building something. Together.

Arric: I'm Proud of Us

I used to think I'd never feel normal again, that I'd always be stuck in the dark.

But I look back now, and I see how far I've come.

I've learned how to speak. How to ask for help. How to sit with my feelings without letting them drown me.

And I'm proud of us. Of my mom. Of myself. Of everyone who didn't give up on me.

We're still learning, still growing, and still healing.

But we're here.

And that means everything.

When His Mind Is Clear

You know, everybody thinks their kid is special in some way. And we are all right. Arric amazes me and others all the time.

Even while he was at the treatment center, once the fog lifted and he started to talk again, the staff would say it was easy to forget why he was there in the first place.

Because when his mind is clear. When he's grounded and back in his rhythm. You see the depth of him, the insight. The way his mind works.

This is a kid who could tell you about stocks and market trends, and other things you wouldn't expect most teenagers to even care about, let alone understand. And he'll say it in such a calm, thoughtful way that you almost forget he's still finding his way back from something heavy.

And sometimes, I even sit back and listen. Because in those moments, he reminds me that the person I've always known is still there. He's still here.

Not just surviving. Not just recovering. But *being*.

Chapter 20: Forever Christmas After

I could tell he was slipping. It wasn't sudden, not a dramatic collapse, but a slow drift I recognized all too well. We tried everything we could to help him get back to baseline before the holiday. Vitamins. Routines. Conversations. Every tool in our emotional and spiritual toolkit. I watched him, hoping for a spark, some sign that he was steadying. But nothing was working. We could see the shift again, slow, subtle at first, but then clearer. And this time, it was right before his son's first Christmas. That timing cut deep. Christmas is supposed to be joy, family, and memory-making.

But instead, we were faced with a choice no parent should ever have to make: keep him home and risk him spiraling deeper, or send him back to the place where healing was possible but where he'd miss the one day that felt sacred to us all.

The decision was made, the bag was packed, and we started the drive back to the place we trusted. It wasn't punishment. It was protection. But it felt like a loss.

We knew what it meant. He would miss Christmas. Miss his baby boy's first Christmas holiday. The pictures. The wrapped toys. The food.

And he knew it too. Somewhere in him, I think he understood. Understood that the best gift he could give his son was a father who was safe, present, and fighting to get better, even if it meant being absent on Christmas morning.

Driving him there that day was one of the heaviest drives of my life. Holiday lights glowed from houses we passed. And here I was, delivering my son back to the place that had become both a refuge and a reminder of everything we were carrying.

After going through the process that I had done so many times, I drove away from that center like I had done so many other times before, tears rolling down my face the whole way home. The Christmas lights blurring through the windshield like a cruel reminder of what we were going to be missing. We kept it small that year. Quiet. The way grief sometimes needs things to be.

The house felt hollow without him.

No big tree. No visitors. Just the three of us. Just the love that still held space for the one who wasn't.

And then, on the other side of all of that, came peace. He was safe. He was seen. He was getting what he needed.

That's the gift I hold onto. The one we'll carry forever.

Because missing one Christmas meant gaining every Christmas after.

Arric: The Return

I knew it was Christmas. I knew I was missing it. And I knew why.

It wasn't like I didn't care. I cared more than I could explain. But my mind wasn't clear enough to hold it all.

I wanted to be home. I wanted to see my son open gifts. I wanted to eat the food and feel the warmth.

But I also knew I wasn't okay. And deep down, I knew being away was the right call.

Still, it hurt. Even through the fog, I felt the ache. The kind that comes from missing something sacred. I remember sitting in that room, thinking I hope they know I'm trying.

Because I was. Even if I couldn't say it. Even if I couldn't show it.

I was trying to come back. Not just for me, but for my son. For my family. For every Christmas after.

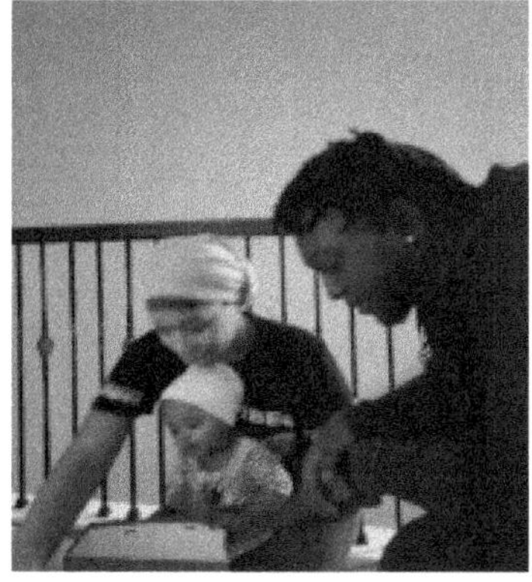

Opening presents after he came home.

• • • •

The next Christmas. Home. Healing. Present

What I Want My Son to Know: *A Letter to Aiden*

THERE ARE THINGS I hope you never have to walk through. But if you ever do, if the world ever feels too loud, if your mind ever gets too heavy, if you ever forget how loved you are, I want you to come back to these words.

You don't have to be perfect to be worthy. You don't have to be strong all the time to be loved. And you never have to hide your truth to belong in this family.

There was a time when I didn't know how to say what I felt. I didn't know how to ask for help. I didn't know how to tell the people who loved me that I was slipping.

But I'm learning. And every day with you helps me build something better. Something more honest. More open. More whole.

I want you to know that softness is not weakness. That crying doesn't make you less of a man. That healing is not shameful. And neither is asking for help.

You are allowed to feel deeply. You are allowed to speak up. You are allowed to change your mind, to grow, to fall, and get back up again.

You are my greatest reminder that the story doesn't end with me. That even when things were hard, love kept going through your mom, through me, and now, through you.

So, if the day ever comes when you question who you are or how to move forward, I want you to remember this: You are not alone. You are not broken. And you are so incredibly loved, just as you are.

Love Always,

Dad

Pray About It, But Also Get Help

"For where two or three are gathered in my name, there am I in the midst of them." Matthew 18:20 (KJV)

God clearly advocates for community. For us to be joined together. For us to help one another.

That includes friends. That includes prayer circles. And yes, that includes therapists.

Because therapy isn't about replacing faith. It's about supporting it.

You can talk to God and talk to a counselor. You can grieve and get grounded. You can pray and process what happened.

Healing isn't meant to happen in isolation. It happens in connection. In courage. In community.

We come from a tradition of faith. Of praying grandmothers and strong mothers who knew how to get a prayer through. And because of that, we've seen miracles. We've felt peace that surpassed understanding. We've known the power of calling on God when nothing else could reach us.

But even in all that knowing, even with all that faith, there are some valleys that prayer alone doesn't pull you out of.

That's not a failure. That's not a lack of faith. That's being human.

Somewhere along the way, in our churches and homes, we were taught that needing help beyond the altar was a weakness. That going to therapy meant you didn't trust God. That taking medication meant you weren't praying hard enough. That grief should be swallowed, depression rebuked, and anxiety ignored in the name of spiritual strength.

But here's what I've learned: You can be drenched in scripture and still drowning in pain. You can be faithful and still fragile. And God, He doesn't shame us for that. He doesn't withhold healing because we sat in a therapist's office. In fact, I believe He often sends help through the very people trained to walk with us when the prayers stop making sense.

Faith and therapy are not enemies. They are partners. And for me, they were both necessary.

There were moments when I could only say, "God, help us," and moments when I had to call someone licensed to do something when I couldn't.

There were moments when I was on my knees, and others when I was filling prescriptions or scheduling appointments.

And I thank God for both.

• • • •

Therapy Isn't a White Thing

LET'S BE REAL: THERAPY has long been seen as something *other people* do. Something reserved for white families. For wealthy folks. For people with the luxury of time.

But that's not true. That's a stigma. And stigma is killing us in silence.

Mental health struggles exist in our communities, too. They live in our homes. In our schools. In our churches. In our sons. In our daughters. In us.

And healing is not disloyalty to your upbringing or your culture. It's an act of love.

Finding a culturally competent therapist. Someone who understands your values, your family dynamics, your background makes all the difference. And they're out there. Black therapists. Brown therapists. Faith-based counselors. People who *see* you.

We say, *"What happens in this house stays in this house,"* but some of what's happening in our homes has to be unlearned. Released. Rewired.

Because silence is not the same as strength. And therapy? Therapy is not a white thing. It's a human thing.

Epilogue: The New Normal

I used to think healing meant getting back to how things were before. That one day we would turn a corner, and it would all be over, like a fever breaking or a bone setting.

But this isn't that kind of journey. With mental illness, there is no "before" to go back to. There's only what we've learned, how we move forward, and what we choose to carry with us.

I started calling it the new normal, even though I didn't like that phrase. It felt like giving in. But over time, I realized it was something more sacred than that. It wasn't giving in; it was growing through. It was survival, love, and faith, redefined.

The truth is, we still have good days. Arric still laughs. He's still annoying like every young male is to his family. He still loves hard. He's still himself, maybe not the exact same version of who he was before this all started, but still fully and beautifully him. The good days aren't always easy, and they don't always come in a row. But they come. And when they do, I cherish them.

I've learned to recognize his baseline. I can tell by the way he eats, the way he talks, how much he sleeps, the look in his eyes, the tone of his voice, if he's drifting. I watch for his habits, is he sleeping too much? Is he isolating? Is his tone sharper than usual? I don't hover, but I pay attention. Because I have to. Because that's what this role now requires of me.

It's no longer about panicking in a moment of crisis; it's about living in a place of gentle awareness. Quiet vigilance. And constant prayer.

There were days when he'd climb into my bed, not saying much, not asking anything. Just lying there because the room felt safe. Because I felt safe. And sometimes I would hold him, or sometimes I'd go lay on the couch and let him rest in peace because he needed it more than I did. That's parenting, in its rawest form, no guidebook, no perfect words, just presence.

There were times when I thought, I'm not equipped for this. I'm not trained for this. But I was wrong. Love is a kind of training. Faith is a kind of training. And watching your child suffer will teach you more about mental health than any textbook ever could.

Even now, I monitor without smothering. I've learned when to check in and when to let space breathe. I've learned how to show up. And I'm still learning.

This is our life now. Not perfect. Not pain-free. But real. And hopeful. And rooted.

This is the new normal.

It's been years since that first night on the couch. Healing didn't make life perfect. It made it honest. And honest love, I've learned, can hold anything- fear, distance, grief, hope...and still make room for joy.

My prayer is that every family who reads this finds their own language for healing. That in every quiet home, what was once hidden finally feels seen. That what was once unspoken becomes understood.

A Letter to My Son

Arric,

I love you. I've always loved you, and I always will. There has never been a day, not one, when I'm not proud to be your mother.

You are strong in ways most people can't understand. You feel deeply, and you love deeply. You care about your friends like they are family. You protect what matters. Even when life tries to dim your light, you keep showing up, even if only in a whisper.

There were moments when I was afraid. Afraid I was losing you. Afraid you were too far away in your mind to ever come back. But you did come back. Piece by piece. And the truth is, you never really left; you were just finding your way through something most people never even talk about.

You've taught me more than I could ever teach you. You've taught me patience, awareness, compassion, and how to really see someone. And I hope you know: no matter what the world says, no matter how hard some days may be, you are never alone.

I am always in your corner.

Love,

Mom

Unspoken, Until Now: Final Words

A Letter to the Ones Still in It

From Me, His Mother

If you're reading this and your child is hurting, if you're sitting in a waiting room or on the other side of a locked door, if you're calling the nurses' station just to hear, "He ate a little more today."

I see you.

I know the fear that lives in your chest. I know the guilt that tries to take root, even when you've done everything right.

I know the guilt that whispers, *"You should have caught this sooner."* I know the ache of loving someone through something you can't fix.

Please hear me. You are not failing. You are standing in the gap. And that is sacred work.

Keep showing up. Keep learning. Keep loving them in the quiet ways, because they feel it even when they can't say it.

When you can't do it alone, reach for help. Call the hotline. Ask the questions. Knock on the doors. Sometimes advocacy looks like persistence. Sometimes it looks like prayer. Sometimes it's both.

Here are a few truths I learned the hard way that I hope will help you:

Write everything down. Dates, names, symptoms. Your notes will matter when memories blur.

Don't wait until the next crisis to prepare. Know your local resources. Save numbers in your phone. Make a safety plan.

Care for yourself, too. You cannot pour from an empty cup. Rest. Cry. Breathe. Allow others to hold you up when you're tired.

Don't let shame silence you. Talking about mental health is not a weakness. It's an act of courage and love.

You're not walking this road alone. And neither is your child.

This road isn't easy. But healing *can* happen. It's slow. It's real. And it's possible.

Shonda Renee

From Me, Arric

If you're the one in the middle of it, if your thoughts are too loud, if the fog feels like it's never going to lift... I know that place.

If you've ever sat in a room full of people and felt invisible, I've been there too.

But I'm still here. And you can be too.

You're not too far gone. You're not broken beyond repair. You're not weak for feeling everything too deeply.

The fog is temporary. Even when it feels permanent, it isn't. You don't have to explain everything perfectly. Just say, *"Something feels off."* That's enough to start.

Ask for help, even if your voice shakes. Needing help doesn't make you weak. It means you're fighting. Your thoughts are not always the truth. Just because your brain tells you something doesn't mean it's real.

Find one anchor. A person, a song, a verse, a memory. Something that reminds you of who you are when you can't see it clearly.

You're still worthy of love. Still worthy of being heard. Still worth fighting for. Hold on, even if it's just by a thread. You're not alone. You're not the only one. And you don't have to stay in the dark.

We made it through a storm we never saw coming. Not perfectly. Not pain-free. But together. And if you're in your storm right now, know, you are not beyond healing.

You are worth the journey back to yourself.

With love,

Arric

Acknowledgements

I want to take a moment to honor some of the incredible people whose compassion and unwavering support made this journey possible. Their kindness gave us strength when we needed it most, and their presence is a reminder that healing is never meant to be walked alone.

There are some people whose kindness and dedication become quiet pillars in the journey toward healing. Though I cannot name everyone who walked alongside us, there are a few who deserve special recognition for the incredible support they gave to Arric and our family during some of our most challenging moments.

Bellaire Behavioral was more than just a facility, it was a refuge where Arric felt safe. Their team showed us, time and time again, what it truly means to care. I will never forget the day they told us they would put a mattress in their day room if they had to, just so Arric would have a place to be during a crisis. That level of compassion made all the difference.

Ms. Jamillah is an extraordinary soul whose care extended far beyond professional boundaries. After a deeply vulnerable session with Arric, she made sure he got home safely, even following him herself. And when a crisis call came after hours, Ms. Caroline answered. I wasn't expecting her to pick up right away, let alone stay on the phone for over an hour-guiding, listening, and supporting in a way only someone with a truly caring heart could.

These moments of human connection reminded me that healing is not a solitary path. It takes a village—hearts willing to show up, to listen, and to walk alongside you. To those who held space for Arric, who saw him when he felt invisible, and who helped us feel less alone, we are forever grateful.

This book would not exist without the love, grace, and strength of so many.

To my son, Arric, thank you for trusting me to share this story. Your honesty, resilience, and quiet strength have taught me more than any degree or life experience ever could. Your story is powerful, and your words will help others heal. I love you endlessly.

To Kamira, thank you for your unwavering love and support for Arric. Your compassion, patience, and understanding have been an answered prayer.

To Aiden, you are the light that reminds us how far we've come and how deeply we love. May your future always reflect the strength that came before you.

To my other children, thank you for your quiet strength, your understanding, and your patience during the times when my focus had to be on your brother. Even in your young adulthood, you carried more than many realized. I am deeply grateful for your grace.

Arrington, while the journey hasn't always been easy, your presence, especially during pivotal moments, made a difference.

To Nick, thank you. You didn't know what was truly happening that night, but you stopped my son from leaving. I don't even want to imagine what could have happened if you hadn't. Because of you, he turned back. Thank you for seeing him, for being present, and for being exactly who we needed in that moment.

To my family, friends, angels, and prayer warriors, thank you for holding me up when I couldn't stand on my own.

And to every nurse, doctor, therapist, caseworker, intake coordinator, and staff member who saw my son as a person and not a chart, thank you. You helped us keep going when we didn't know how.

To the parents who are still in it- the waiting rooms, the phone calls, the quiet terror of not knowing, this book is for you.

To every Black mother, Black father, and family who has been told to stay silent:

You don't have to anymore. Healing belongs to us, too.

And above all, to God, thank You for breath, for strength, for moments of clarity when I couldn't think straight. Thank You for holding my son in ways I never could, and for holding me when I was falling apart.

This story is not just mine. It's Yours.

Action Resources: Start Here

Small steps that can make a big difference:

- Save 988 in your phone right now (Suicide & Crisis Lifeline).

- Identify one safe person you can call when things feel heavy.

- Create a "calm corner" at home, a space with something comforting (a blanket, journal, music, scripture, or photo).

- Schedule one check-in a week with yourself: *How am I eating? Sleeping? Feeling?* Write it down.

- Have a family code word or phrase that signals "I need help" without needing to explain.

Healing doesn't start with doing everything at once. It starts with one choice, one step, one moment of courage at a time.

Emergency & Mental Health Crisis Hotlines

988 Suicide & Crisis Lifeline

- **Call or Text:** 988

- **Website:** 988lifeline.org[1]

- Available 24/7 for anyone in emotional distress or suicidal crisis. Also offers support for concerned family/friends.

Crisis Text Line

- **Text:** HOME to **741741**

- **Website:** crisistextline.org[2]

---

1. https://988lifeline.org

- Free, confidential support by text message for any mental health or emotional crisis.

National Alliance on Mental Illness (NAMI) HelpLine

- **Call:** 1-800-950-NAMI (6264)
- **Text:** "HelpLine" to 62640
- **Website:** nami.org/help
- Open M–F, 10am–10pm EST. Offers resources, education, and peer support.

SAMHSA National Helpline (Substance Abuse & Mental Health Services Administration)

- **Call:** 1-800-662-HELP (4357)
- **Website:** samhsa.gov/find-help/national-helpline
- 24/7 free treatment referrals and information for individuals and families facing mental health or substance use disorders.

The Steve Fund (Mental health support for young people of color)

- **Text:** STEVE to **741741**
- **Website:** stevefund.org[3]
- Dedicated to supporting the mental health of Black, Indigenous, and students of color.

Mental Health Resources for Our Community

---

2. https://www.crisistextline.org

3. https://www.stevefund.org

Because healing takes faith, support, and the right tools.

Therapy for Black Girls www.therapyforblackgirls.com[4]

A directory to find culturally competent therapists and mental wellness content tailored for Black women and girls.

Therapy for Black Men www.therapyforblackmen.org[5]

A safe space for Black men seeking mental health support, resources, and therapist access.

Inclusive Therapists www.inclusivetherapists.com[6]

Centers the needs of marginalized populations and offers a directory of inclusive, affirming therapists.

The Boris Lawrence Henson Foundation www.borislhensonfoundation.org[7]

Founded by Taraji P. Henson, this organization provides mental health resources and services for the Black community.

Open Path Collective www.openpathcollective.org[8]

Affordable mental health care options, including many culturally sensitive therapists offering reduced rates.

Faith + Mental Health Resources

The Loveland Foundation www.thelovelandfoundation.org[9]

Provides therapy support specifically for Black women and girls, with a focus on healing from trauma.

My Wellbeing www.mywellbeing.com[10]

Matches people with therapists based on shared values, including spirituality and cultural background.

Faithful Counseling www.faithfulcounseling.com[11]

---

4. https://www.therapyforblackgirls.com
5. https://www.therapyforblackmen.org
6. https://www.inclusivetherapists.com
7. https://www.borislhensonfoundation.org
8. https://www.openpathcollective.org
9. https://www.thelovelandfoundation.org
10. https://www.mywellbeing.com

Offers Christian-based therapy from licensed professionals who respect and integrate faith.

Support Apps & Tools

Shine App – Mental wellness and daily check-ins created by women of color

Liberate App – Meditation and mindfulness for the Black community

Safe Place App – Mental health education, resources, and self-care tips for the Black community

11. https://www.faithfulcounseling.com

About the Author

Shonda Renee *is a public safety leader, writer, and advocate who shares her personal journey of parenting through crisis with honesty and grace. She created this journal to offer comfort, clarity, and community to others navigating similar paths. Through her work in leadership and lived experience, she hopes to make healing conversations more accessible*

Arric Strickland*, whose voice appears throughout Unspoken Until Now, shares deeply from his own experiences with mental health, hospitalization, and hope. His reflections serve as a powerful reminder that healing is possible- and that love, when met with honesty, can open doors to new beginnings.*

www.ingramcontent.com/pod-product-compliance
Lightning Source LLC
LaVergne TN
LVHW011049110826
845149LV00015B/3424